Contents

Children
about the house

Hilary Gelson

a Design Centre book

Children about the house
First edition published 1976
A Design Centre book published by
Design Council 28 Haymarket
London SW1Y 4SU

Designed by Anne Fisher
Illustrated by Derek Higley,
Michael McCarthy, Michelle Mortimer,
Ann Winterbotham
Printed and bound by Martin Cadbury
Limited, Hylton Road, Worcester
WR2 5JU

ISBN O 85072 024 9
© Design Council 1976

Living with children

Toys littering the living room, prams in the hall, nappies strung across the bathroom and a copy of Dr Spock on the kitchen table .... It all adds up to the chaos of modern living with children. It seems that, after centuries of relative neglect and absentee parenthood, children now dominate the average household and intrude on our adult world to an extent that would have horrified and enraged our forbears.

Does this new style of family life reflect changing attitudes on the part of modern parents, or is it the result of the activities of our professional architects and house planners? Either way it certainly appears that most family homes in Britain are highly inadequate machines for us to live in. Most are devoid of child proof safety devices, proper storage facilities and easily cleaned wall and floor surfaces. Ill-planned interiors make it impossible for parents to control clutter or escape from noise, and very few houses provide for a changing pattern of life as the family grows.

But we manage, and even if we cannot alter the basic structure of our homes at least we can reorganise their interiors to meet some of the problems of living with young children—and that is what this book is all about. It is a chronological survey of the developing needs and design requirements of children about the house, starting from the day they come home from the maternity hospital up to the moment they reach the comparative independence of their first term at infant school.

Equipment for a first nursery

The first thing to prepare for your baby's arrival will be the nursery, and you can happily escape from many long and dreary hours of pregnancy with plans and ideas for equipping and decorating this important new room. Before you embark on the enjoyable tasks of planning a colour scheme and choosing furnishing fabrics and finishes, it is essential to decide what equipment you are likely to need in your nursery area. Don't underestimate the size of this task—you will be bombarded with conflicting advice from friends and retailers, and you will find a bewilderingly wide selection of nursery goods in the shops to choose from.

Cost will inevitably dictate most of your decisions, but you should also consider other important criteria such as safety and durability. You will often find designs that conform to accepted British Standards, and some manufacturers of nursery equipment have taken part in the British Standards Institution's 'Kitemark' scheme. This means that their products are tested for durability, efficiency and safety (where applicable) and it is certainly worth looking for the Kitemark label on any product you buy. You can also look for well designed children's toys and nursery equipment in the Design Council's Design Index, which contains photographs and descriptions of a wide range of products selected on the grounds of safety, reliability, good value and appearance.

Clothes to begin with

Improved home laundry facilities, coupled with the introduction of plastics, quick-drying and easy-care fabrics, and stretch towelling suits, have led to a completely new concept of a baby's layette. In the first months all you really need is a minimum of three complete changes of clothing, together with some warm garments for use out of doors. The following list is based on minimum quantities and compiled from my personal experience that the less you have, the less you need.

Three cotton vests Choose vests with envelope necks rather than the tie-front kind. They fit better and are easier to put on a very young baby.

Six stretch towelling suits A stretch suit is ideal for small babies. It is warm, gives plenty of freedom of movement, and the built-in mittens prevent the baby from scratching his face. For safety, always check that the foot is loose around the toes. If tight it can cause deformed toes and ingrowing toe-nails. Later on, if the suit is still wearable but the feet are too small, cut them off and use socks instead.

Three cardigans Choose natural wool for preference since some babies are allergic to synthetic fibres. Check that the cardigans have deep raglan arm holes or wide inset sleeves to avoid restricting movement or circulation. Avoid lacy patterns that can catch and damage a baby's fingers and make sure that all buttons and ribbons are sewn on firmly.

Two bonnets Fussy but necessary in the early months.

One woollen shawl or lightweight cellular blanket

Two cotton shawls These should be lightweight and are for indoor use. They are particularly handy for wrapping the baby securely in his cradle.

Two warm sleeping suits These are useful for pram outings in cold weather. If your baby is born in the autumn it is worth buying a lightweight quilted nylon carrycot. These are excellent for keeping the baby warm and secure when travelling and can be carried straight from the nursery to the pram or carry-cot. Remember though, that they are safe only for very young babies who are unable to sit up.

Six pairs waterproof pants During the early weeks the pull-on elasticated kind are easier to put on than those with snap fasteners.

Disposable liners These add to the baby's comfort and help to prevent heavy soiling of the outer nappy.

Twenty-four towelling nappies There are two main types of nappy—washable and disposable. If you buy washable nappies buy the best you can afford; they will certainly last longer and can be kept for a second baby. Disposable nappies, on the other hand, save a lot of washing and are very useful when travelling.

Twelve muslin squares Although not essential, these are particularly useful as bibs, clothes protectors and mopping-up cloths after a feed. They make a good comforter later on as well.

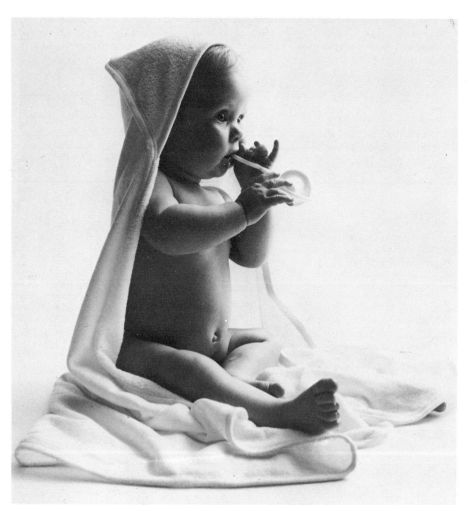

Bathing

Although a baby **bath** has a relatively short life in the nursery – three or four months at the most – it is much more practical for the inexperienced mother to use a portable bath and stand that can be assembled in the warmth of a nursery area, rather than bend over the side of the family bath tub. It can also be useful later on for storing toys or encouraging water play away from the busy kitchen sink area. There are several designs on the market to choose from. Points to look for are a sloping base which supports the baby's back and allows the mother to use both hands, and enough depth for kicking and splashing. You can buy baths which have a folding stand, equipped with a towel rail, which also doubles as a carry-cot or crib stand, and this is certainly a useful extra. Other bathtime accessories include a rubber **safety mat** to prevent slipping, a plastic backed towelling **apron** and a soft bath **towel**, preferably with a hood, which is large enough to envelop the baby, but still manageable for the mother.

Sleeping

A lined wicker **cradle** or **crib** is very practical for the first months and, since the latter weeks of pregnancy are a good time for sewing, many mothers-to-be simply need to buy or borrow a wicker frame (usually with a stand) and some suitable lining material. The lining must be detachable for washing and should preferably be an easy-care fabric.

When it comes to choosing a **mattress** you are sure to be given some conflicting advice. Many child health experts believe that the traditional horse-hair mattress is safer since it allows air to circulate freely. It is, however, significantly less hygienic than washable, lightweight plastics foam, which also gives good support to the baby's back. Whichever type of mattress you choose, you will also need two rubber sheets and at least two or three of each of the following, which can double up for use in the pram:
Lightweight wool blankets The air-pocket variety is very good.
Cotton top sheets
Fitted bottom sheets, preferably stretch towelling.

Pillows should never be used with small babies under a year old because of the danger of smothering. Pillows for older children should be made to the British Standard BS 4578 which requires a curled hair filling. This is very porous and can easily be washed and dried.

An item of equipment for which British Standards are particularly useful is the **carry-cot.** When selecting a design, check that the material used is harmless, corrosion resistant and fire inhibiting. Handles should be placed so that the carry-cot can be moved easily and steadily, and any stand that you use should not be less than three-quarters the length of the carry-cot and should be wider than it to ensure complete stability. You should also check on the weight it can safely hold and make certain that any separate components fit firmly in place.

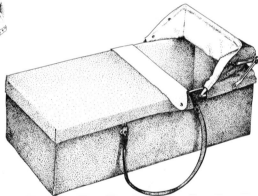

Although some mothers prefer to use a **cot** from the very first weeks, the majority wait until their babies are four or five months old. As the cot is one of the longest lasting and hardest used items in the nursery, it pays to be particularly vigilant and discriminating when choosing a suitable design. Points to look out for include rigid, strong construction and secure, child-proof catch fasteners for the drop side. The distance between the vertical bars should not be greater than about 80mm and the height of the top rail above the mattress base should be about 700mm with a mattress depth of not more than 100mm. If the cot has a painted or lacquered finish it must not contain dangerous quantities of lead or other poisonous substances—this is particularly important if you are buying a second-hand cot or re-painting an old one. The majority of cots on the market today are manufactured to BSI standards and should therefore be marked with the appropriate number. For standard domestic designs this is BS 1753 and you should make sure that any new cot you buy is marked accordingly.

Although useful in a large household, a **baby alarm** can hardly be considered an essential item of nursery equipment. It only increases parental anxiety by transmitting every snuffle and whimper and, anyway, most mothers seem to have a sixth sense when it comes to hearing a cry for attention. If the nursery is sited some distance away, however, an alarm system is useful, as well as reassuring, to the inexperienced parent and it can always be used later on as an intercom system between floors.

Nappy changing

A well-organised nappy changing area is essential, not only for new mothers (and fathers) who are nervous of the task, but also from the long-term point of view because the routine will continue for at least a couple of years. There are several decisions to be made before you start choosing the equipment you need. First of all, if space is at a premium in the nursery you may need to make a changing area in the bathroom—and in some ways this is a more practical idea since there is a constant water supply. On the other hand, it is rare to find sufficient storage space in the average family bathroom for clean nappies, toiletries and other essentials. Perhaps the best answer is a folding changing table in the nursery, and you can now buy designs with a safe padded foam changing surface, drawers, a towel rail and a shelf. Alternatively you can make a mobile changing trolley from an ordinary wooden trolley by equipping it with a towel rail, some drawers and a sturdy melamine tray and work top. But

be careful never to leave a baby unattended on this type of changing surface.

In addition to a suitable changing surface and a foam padded mat you will need two **buckets** of about fifteen litres capacity with closely fitting lids. One will be for soiled nappies, which should be kept in a strong **disinfectant solution.** There are several brands of disinfectant available which contain anti-bacterial and cleansing agents to protect the baby from nappy rash. The second bucket is for soiled liners, disposable nappies (if you use them), cotton wipes and other waste. It is a good idea for this bucket to have space for an air freshener.

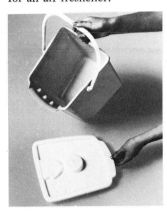

Feeding and meals

Before you choose **feeding equipment** you must decide how and where you plan to feed your baby. Breast-feeding mothers will have relatively little to buy and the feeding routine can be carried out almost anywhere. Bottle-fed babies, on the other hand, need a certain amount of special equipment that generally ends up in the kitchen where there are already facilities for boiling water, making up feeds and storing bottles at a safe temperature. If you can afford it, and if there is enough space in the nursery, a kitchen-style working unit complete with hot-plate, sink, a small refrigerator and a cupboard store is obviously the ideal solution.

Wherever you decide to prepare the feeds you will certainly need the following equipment:

One plastics sterilising container with lid You may be able to save money here by buying a simple five litre plastics container with a lid.

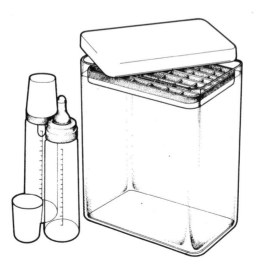

Four feeding bottles These should be about 220g capacity with feeder caps. They should be made of non-breakable polycarbonate plastics and should have a wide neck for easy washing and filling.

Four teats

Nylon bottle brush with a non-rust handle

Sterilising solution There are several excellent products that can be used for sterilising feeding equipment without boiling and are safe and effective. One type comes in tablet form which is simpler to use, particularly for travelling when the risk of infection is greater.

Measuring jug This should be clearly marked and at least one litre capacity.

Plastics tongs These are for removing items from the steriliser.

Bottle warmer Although not essential, this is a useful piece of equipment, particularly for early morning feeds in winter when you can wait in a warm nursery rather than in a cold kitchen for the bottle to reach the right temperature. Make sure that the design you buy is double-insulated for safety with a two-core flex.

Nursing chair Again, not essential, but it is very important to feel comfortable and relaxed when feeding your baby. Many mothers recommend a rocking chair, but make sure that the height of the arm is right for the feeding position.

As soon as your baby can sit up he will need a **high chair.** Once again, this is a long-lived piece of nursery equipment, so take care when you are shopping for a suitable design. First make sure that the construction is generally good and that the chair cannot tip up when weight is put on the feeding tray or the arms. It is best to choose one with a detachable feeding tray that can be washed after every meal. If possible, find a multipurpose design that converts into a low-level chair and table for use in the nursery later on. You can now buy designs that incorporate a traditional wooden high chair complete with detachable feeding tray, safety strap and foot rest, combined with a high dining chair, a low feeding chair, a stool and a nursery table—all within one basic unit. They may not look as attractive as my own Victorian high chair, but they are infinitely more practical and versatile.

You should also be very selective when it comes to choosing **nursery tableware.** There is a wealth of special cups, plates and cutlery on the market today, all of which is ostensibly designed to help your baby to feed himself. In my experience, however, all you need is a lidded beaker in transparent plastics so that you can see the liquid level as you help the baby to use it; a plastics plate with a suction base, preferably without divisions—they encourage young children to be even more choosy about their food; and a small plastics spoon and fork set.

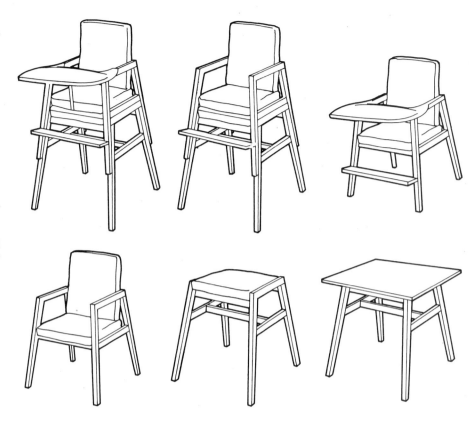

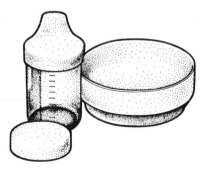

Clothes protectors are an essential part of nursery feeding equipment and, although there are several ways of dealing with the problem of spills at mealtimes, I have yet to find a cover that successfully protects both clothes and the floor around a high chair. A

plastics bib with a trough at the bottom to catch the food is one solution, but they are not too comfortable to wear and tend to hamper the child in a high chair where there is little space between him and the edge of the tray. A large plastics-backed towelling bib is much more comfortable and quite hygienic, but the plastics surface has a fairly short life and, although the bib may absorb liquids, it does not cope with solid food. Perhaps the only answer is a heavy polythene sheet under the high chair together with a soft, absorbent towelling cover-up. This way the floor is protected and the child has a comfortable meal.

First play

Babies enjoy looking at moving shapes and bright colours from a very early age, so a comfortable **reclining chair** is an important item of nursery equipment. It provides a safe play seat and is also extremely useful for the busy mother and when travelling. There are several flexible designs available, most of which have a stand so that you can convert the seat easily into a swing or a high chair. Other accessories include feeding trays, carrying handles and special hooks for clipping the chair over the back of conventional restaurant or dining chairs.

Look for a chair that will adjust from the nearly horizontal position suitable for a young baby to a vertical seat for a toddler, with a foam-padded cushion covered in machine-washable terry-towelling or something similar. This will be more comfortable and hygienic for the baby in hot weather. The play potential of a reclining chair for a young baby is considerable. It can be placed under a mobile indoors, or out in the garden during the summer, and a detachable tray makes a useful small play table. It is also light enough to carry about the house, so there is no reason for the baby ever to be left unattended while you get on with the household chores. Take great care, however, not to put the chair near the edge of a table or near dangerous equipment in the kitchen. It is wise to use a separate harness as an added safety precaution.

Before you buy or borrow a **playpen,** think whether you really need one. Remember that it will take up valuable indoor storage space and that, provided that your play room is child-proof—which it will certainly need to be once your baby is walking—there is no reason to keep him in a playpen at an earlier age. On the other hand, if you have a large house or flat it is virtually impossible to ensure that every part of it is safe for an adventurous eight month old and that all your own treasures are out of reach. In this case it may be a good idea to get a lightweight design that you can move easily from room to room. The circular folding variety, complete with raised floor, fine netting enclosure and plastics top rail, usually weighs about 7 kg and is much more easily assembled than the traditional wooden type. If you inherit or buy a second-hand playpen, make sure that the distance between the bars is no more than 80 mm and that the surfaces are painted with non-toxic paint or varnish.

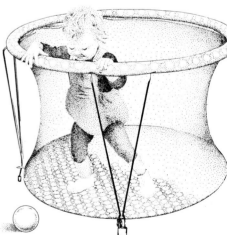

The nursery interior

As soon as you have drawn up a check-list of basic nursery equipment, you can begin to examine the potential of your nursery area in terms of storage, heating, lighting and wall and floor surface treatments.

Storage

Well designed storage is essential in a nursery, where clothes, toys, books and treasures all have to be kept within easy reach. In order to work out how much storage you need, start by making a complete list of all the clothes and equipment you will have to keep in the room. Remember that you will have to find space later on for discarded items, such as baby clothes and outgrown toys, as well as for an ever-increasing amount of hobby and sports equipment after the children start school. Nursery storage should ideally be capable of developing with the needs of the child, so I would strongly advise against buying small-scale furniture that may look pretty and be practical for the first year or so, but will soon prove inadequate and a waste of money. Instead, make the most of the available wall space and follow a vertical storage plan so that toys can be stored at low level, with bed linen, clothes and books above the reach of the very young, and out-of-season garments, outgrown equipment and everything else firmly stowed away in top cupboards. Next, you must decide whether to invest in built-in storage or a free-standing arrangement of shelves and cupboards. Built-in storage furniture has many advantages, particularly in a nursery area where it takes up less floor space and tends to be cheaper than ready-made wardrobes and chests of drawers. In my experience, an inexpensive **assemble-yourself system** incorporating adjustable shelving, pullout trays, low-level lockers and sufficient hanging space for a developing wardrobe, is an excellent solution to the problem.

Heating

A thermostatically-controlled household central heating system is obviously the best and safest method of maintaining a warm, steady temperature in the nursery. This is particularly important in any room used by a very young baby, since the newly born can develop a condition known as hypothermia if nursed at a temperature much below 18°C. The nursery must therefore be kept at a constant day and night temperature of between 18°C and 21°C and, to ensure this, it is advisable to install a wall thermometer in the room and experiment with the temperature control switch on your heating system until you find the setting which will maintain the correct temperature level.

If you do not live in a centrally heated house or flat, there are many other methods of direct heating available, but do make sure that the heater you buy meets the required safety standards and is well protected. If you plan to use a wall-mounted gas or electric fire, for example, it must be protected with a fixed guard, manufactured to British Standards specifications and marked with the BS number 3140. This design covers the whole fire, not just the heating element, and is fitted with side clips which are impossible for a child to unfasten. An oil heater should always be filled out of doors and placed on a sheet of non-combustible material, well out of draughts and away from curtains or furniture. It should if possible be a design approved by the Oil Appliance Manufacturers Association. Finally, free-standing convector heaters should be stable and have a safety cut-off switch which operates automatically if the airflow is restricted in any way or if the heater is knocked over. Check also that the air vents are small enough to prevent a child from pushing objects through on to the element and that the heater is properly earthed with a three-core flex.

Lighting

Good night lighting is important in a nursery area, not only to reassure the young, but to help parents who are disturbed during the night by a hungry baby, or later by a wakeful child. One of the most successful solutions to the problem is to install a dimmer control switch for an existing light fitting. At the lowest level it provides a constant glow in the room and, if it is necessary to feed or change the baby during the night, you can increase the light slowly, without disturbing him. It is perhaps worth adding that you should remember to switch off the light in the morning—it is not always easy to notice on a bright morning, particularly during the summer.

Windows

Windows are a potential hazard in any room used by a young child, and particularly so in a nursery where children are left alone in the early morning and afternoon rest periods. Wherever the nursery is situated—even if it is at basement or ground-floor level —it is essential to install a safety locking device to prevent an accidental fall. The type of lock or bolt you need will depend largely on the design of your nursery window. There are window stops available, for example, that secure sliding sash windows and, at the same time, provide adequate ventilation in the room; locking window catches for wooden casement frames; and window restrictor stay mechanisms suitable for top hung windows. Since window locks are also an essential part of crime prevention, it is a good idea to call in or consult a security locksmith in your area to help you find the correct type of lock. Alternatively, you can buy an adjustable window guard, designed with vertical window bars and a locking mechanism that can be operated quickly by an adult in the event of a fire.

Curtains and blinds

An increasing number of retail shops are now stocking ranges of flameproofed or flame resistant furnishing textiles and it is obviously much safer to choose this type of material when selecting curtains or blinds for the nursery, as well as for the rest of the house. Certainly, you should avoid materials that have a rapid spread of flame, such as lightweight cottons, rayons and mixtures of these two fibres. Bonded linings are generally not flame retardant, so you should consider this when choosing a suitable lining material. Lined curtains, however, are preferable in a nursery, where it is important to be able to keep out natural daylight during the summer, as well as insulating the room from draughts during the winter. If you prefer blinds—

which are much cheaper and if carefully made will fit the window closely—I would suggest using a spongeable, laminated fabric that retains its shape and good looks longer than loosely woven material.

Floors

Nursery flooring must be durable, easy to clean and comfortable to play on. The surface should be capable of withstanding potty accidents, sickness and paint spills, as well as providing scope for toy train enthusiasts, mini-car racing drivers and wheeled traffic of all kinds. This virtually eliminates a soft floor-covering—at least for the first two years or so—for although warm, safe and comfortable to crawl on, a fitted carpet is unhygienic and difficult to maintain. Equally, loose rugs scattered over a hard floor surface such as wood blocks or ceramic tiles are particularly dangerous in a nursery area. The safest solution to the problem is to choose a semi-hard floor covering such as linoleum sheet, vinyl asbestos or cork tiles. You can now buy textured sheet vinyl, for instance, which is warm and pleasant to walk on with bare feet and is simple to install. From the maintenance point of view, it only needs regular brushing and a mop with a mild detergent. Alternatively, sealed cork tiles provide a warm, comfortable floor surface in a neutral colour, which is easier to integrate into a decoration scheme and less demanding on the eye than a patterned floor covering. If you cannot afford to cover an existing slippery hard floor surface, remove the old polish with white spirit and coat the surface with a plastic resin non-slip floor seal.

Walls

Before you tackle the problem of selecting a suitable wall finish, it is important to understand how a young child regards the walls of his nursery.

During the early months, walls represent security and are an important source of visual stimulation to the baby in his crib. With increased mobility, however, they represent a barricade—isolation from mother and the rest of the household. The young child, therefore, feels that he must control these vertical obstacles, first by touching and familiarising himself with their surface pattern and texture and, later, by adding his own contribution to the decorative content of a wall-paper pattern—I deal with combating this particular temptation in a subsequent chapter. Since we are concerned here with the needs of the under twos, I would advice you to choose a robust, easy to clean wall covering such as vinyl or gloss paint.

The wall around the cot is particularly vulnerable, since it is an easily accessible play surface in the early morning waking hours and may also need to be washed frequently during a period of sickness.

When it comes to deciding between a patterned wall covering or a plain one there are no strict rules. On the whole, young children identify strongly with the garish transfers that seem to decorate the majority of nursery equipment on the market today and, although you may not admire this type of design, your child will almost certainly prefer a jungle pattern of animals and flowers to a plain paper of your own choice. There is some evidence to suggest that even very young babies can benefit from the visual stimulation provided by a brightly patterned paper.

Finally, one cannot consider a colourful wall treatment without reference to nursery colour schemes in general. Since this is probably the only opportunity you will have of decorating your child's room, without considering his own tastes and wishes, I suppose it is very much a question of how you visualise an ideal nursery area, in terms of colour, pattern, pictures and general decoration. The important thing to remember is that you are going to spend a lot of time in the room for the first year or so, so don't choose a wallpaper design that you will tire of easily or colours that will appear harsh and unfriendly in the early mornings.

Coping in a small space

If you are forced, by lack of space, to share a bedroom with your new baby you should consider the advantages of such an arrangement, rather than look ahead to the problems that will arise later on. Most nursing mothers find it much more convenient to have the crib near their own bed; anxious parents are spared the effort of getting up in the night to check on the baby's well-being, and it is also cheaper during the winter months to heat one room than two. It is essential though to achieve a degree of privacy in any shared space and, if you plan the area carefully, this can be obtained for comparatively little cost. At the same time, you will need to decentralise nursery activities and related equipment to other areas of the house. The nappy-changing routine, for example, can be carried out in the bathroom, feeding equipment can be kept in the kitchen and your living area will inevitably become the place for playing in as soon as your baby becomes mobile.

Basic equipment
It is important to remember that the space requirements of a young baby are minimal. A small cot, a storage unit and

a comfortable nursing chair are all that will be required in terms of basic nursery furniture. Of course, you can make do with even less—babies have been known to sleep perfectly well in a converted laundry basket or bottom drawer—but I have found that one or two well-chosen items of equipment make life much easier for the harassed mother. At a pinch they can always be obtained second-hand through your local clinic, from a jumble sale, charity shop, or through friends.

A **carry-cot** with folding transporter is an essential piece of equipment, particularly if you are living in a small flat and there is nowhere to store a pram at ground-floor level. Many mothers, however, prefer to use an ordinary cot or crib at night, since this is the longest sleep period and the air circulates more freely in them than in a plastic lined carry-cot. In this case, I would advise a **folding canvas bed** rather than a conventional Moses basket

Left: The only special design problem in a shared nursery parents' bedroom is in achieving an adequate degree of privacy for both parents and baby. In this plan the cot is located well away from draughts and the main circulation pattern of the parents' bedroom. Suspended ceiling blinds, teamed with a free-standing storage unit which doubles up as a useful worktop dressing surface, create visual privacy alongside the parents' sleeping area. The louvred screen not only acts as an efficient draught excluder, but adds to the feeling of warmth and security within the nursery area. The pendant light fittings are controlled by a dimmer switch alongside the parents' bed and heating is supplied by a thermostatically controlled system. The cheerfully decorated window blind, wall paper and cot provide visual interest for both baby and parents, as does the red plastics wall pocket holding favourite toys and everyday essentials.

or lined crib. It will last longer, can easily be wheeled into another room if necessary and will prove useful later on when travelling with a toddler.

A **drawer storage unit** with sufficient space for a complete change of clothing, together with spare sheets and blanket for the cot, is all you really need in a shared sleeping area as the rest can be kept in a separate clothes or airing cupboard. Apart from folded clothes, however, you will also need to store things like socks, shoes, and a hairbrush, and a strong **canvas wall pocket** alongside the dressing area is an excellent solution to the problem of storing these small bits and pieces easily and accessibly.

Feeding equipment
In many ways it is more convenient to keep sterilising and feeding equipment in the kitchen, where there are built-in facilities for boiling water, washing bottles and so on. I would suggest, therefore, that you reserve one shelf in a cupboard next to the sink for storing milk formula, sterilising tablets and canned baby foods and keep the sterilising unit nearby. In this way you can carry out both the sterilising and bottle-making routines in one area of the kitchen. You should, however,

make sure that the cupboard space is dry and well insulated from a steamy kitchen.

Toy storage
Toy storage can present a considerable problem in a small living area, particularly when it comes to wheeled toys such as tricycles, doll's prams or wheel barrows. In my own double-duty living area, I have a wicker laundry basket at one end as a main storage depot for frequently used toys; wheeled traffic is stowed over-night in the hall cupboard; and easily mislaid jigsaw puzzles, play bricks and construction kit components are kept in draw-string bags on the back of the cupboard door. If you have enough wall space and can afford it, it is worth buying a wall storage unit for the living area that will house your own possessions at high level and has sufficient cupboard space below for stowing books and toys. I suggest cupboards rather than open shelves here, since it is almost impossible to store toys tidily and a cupboard door will successfully conceal the chaos.

A combined bedroom/playroom

It is reasonable to assume that, by the time a first child is two-and-a-half or three years old, a second baby will have joined the 'first nursery'. You will therefore have to reorganise the room to provide for the sleeping, storage and play requirements of two children, creating a shared bedroom/play area that will cater for the indoor activities of a pre-school child, as well as for the needs of a young baby.

Sleeping arrangements

It is important to look ahead when it comes to deciding on the size and type of **bed** that will be suitable for a child who has finally outgrown his cot. When it comes to planning for two children, obviously the best solution is to invest in sturdy, adult-sized **bunk beds,** equipped with good quality mattresses. They are space-saving, will provide endless play value in the early years and should last

until the children have grown up. Later on, the beds can be split up for use in separate bedrooms and when the children eventually leave home they can always be used in a guest room. There are many different designs to choose from, but you should beware of the cheaper varieties, which can prove unstable and are often not equipped with an adequate safety rail at top level. Other features to check on include: the distance between the top and bottom bunks, as ideally a parent should be able to sit comfortably and read a bedtime story; low level storage provision, either in the form of mobile lockers or pull-out drawers; and lastly that mattresses are firm and of good quality to provide correct postural support over the years.

At the same time, you should not ignore the considerable play potential of bunk beds. Try fixing a pair of roller blinds to the side edge of the top bunk —they will swiftly transform the lower section into a house/boat/train/shop and provide many hours of imaginative play in the bedroom area. There are, however, certain drawbacks to bunk beds, principally because they create an immediate sense of hierarchy in the nursery, and will probably be the cause of many a battle over who should be allowed to sleep on top. The only solution is to impose a strict rotation rule. For example, 'all change' once a week, but it is perhaps worth pointing out to the tearful occupant of the bottom bunk the advantages of having a table alongside the bed, access to 'secret' drawers below and the possibility of gathering all his favourite toys and books around him. You may well find that your children prefer to keep to their own territory rather than change regularly, and will come to an amicable agreement with much less trouble than you expected.

Alternatively, if you have plenty of space you may decide to buy a simple **divan bed,** or at least wait until your

second child is older before investing in bunk beds. On the whole, I would advise against buying an extending design or so-called 'cot-bed' with removable sides. Both require special-sized bedding and a cot-bed will only last for five or six years. The best answer is a sturdy adult-sized divan bed, preferably equipped with low-level storage for bedding during the day-time. It should be placed in a corner or alongside one wall for extra protection for a restless sleeper and in this way you can keep the centre floor area free for play activities.

Above and right: 'Kidplace,' designed by Maynard Hale Lyndon for Placemakers, Cambridge, Massachusetts, USA, must be one of the most ingenious bunk bed systems on the market today, with its built-in puppet theatre/shop, ship's ladder and fortresslike construction. The designer has also paid special attention to frequently forgotten details such as the height between the two bed platforms—an adult can sit on the bottom bed to read a goodnight story or change a sheet without bumping his head. And there is adjacent storage space on both levels for dolls and books, a clock or night light, as well as additional screened surfaces for pinboard space.

Bedmaking

The daily task of making children's beds—particularly bunk beds—is considerably eased if you invest in **fitted sheets** and a **continental quilt** or duvet right from the start. Terylene fibre-filled quilts are warm, lightweight, and machine washable, and are therefore more suitable for young children than the more expensive feather and down-filled varieties. Apart from the quilt you will need at least two covers, preferably in easy-care fabric, and a pair of fitted bottom sheets. You can now buy stretch towelling glove sheets in seven sizes, ranging from the cradle to an adult-sized bunk bed and, although the initial investment in bedding may seem high it will certainly prove worthwhile particularly when it comes to encouraging children to make their own beds. They will soon learn how easy it is to shake out a duvet rather than strip and re-make an entire bed. This type of bedding can also be easily stored in low-level drawers or lockers when not in use, transforming the bedroom into a day-time activity space rather than just a place for sleeping in.

Ample storage

The success of any double-duty interior invariably depends on the extent of its storage, and this is particularly important in a shared bedroom/play area, where clothes, shoes, books, toys and nursery equipment must be neatly stowed away to ensure a clutter-free floor area for children's play activities.

The arrival of a second baby in the nursery inevitably means a re-assessment of any existing storage facilities in the room, for you will have to re-introduce certain items of nursery equipment, as well as providing for the developing clothes, books and toys of an older child. This may simply involve the addition of extra shelves and low-level cupboards to an existing wall storage unit in the room. Alternatively, you may have to re-think your storage provision entirely if you have earlier decided to make do with a small cupboard and

chest of drawers. In this case, I would advise you to install a modular wall unit system incorporating a full length cupboard with an interior that can be arranged to include a two-tier system of rails to allow sufficient hanging space for both children's clothes in the early years. The system should also have plenty of adjustable shelving—lower shelves for books and the higher shelves for treasures and collections well out of the reach of the youngest child. Lastly, the lower section should include a series of lockers and pull-out trays.

Heavy duty plastics trays can be used as low-level stacking drawers in a wall storage unit and can be easily pulled out during play activities. A cheaper alternative is to use plastics washing up bowls—ideal, in my experience, for stowing small cars, doll's house equipment and play bricks—or plastics containers designed for storing domestic

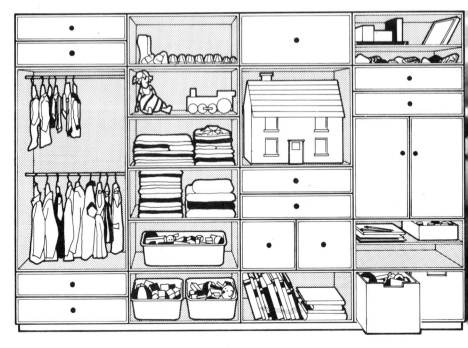

This simple play table designed by Maynard Hale Lyndon for Placemakers, Cambridge, Massachusetts, USA, incorporates a spacious working surface complete with adjacent storage for painting and craft materials. The lower bins can be used to provide easily accessible stowing space for toys, so creating a shared storage unit for all age groups.

cleaning materials, These are usually equipped with a carrying handle and are divided into fist-sized compartments which are very good for storing construction kits, jigsaw puzzles or bricks.

Choosing furniture

Although I would strongly advise against buying small-scale storage furniture for children's rooms, it is important to provide some loose furniture that they can relate to, in terms of scale, design and interpretation. This need not be expensive, despite the high price of much of the purpose-made children's furniture available today. For example, two or three mini wicker chairs plus a sturdy table with legs cut down to size are really all you need. Alternatively, I have found that folding picnic furniture is extremely practical and can also be used for many other purposes around the house and garden. Lightweight aluminium framed tables with a non-slip work top and safe contoured edges, provide an excellent low-level surface for assembling construction kits or sorting out a jig saw puzzle. At the end of the day, they can be folded up and stowed under a bed or inside a cupboard near the play area. Similarly, you can buy tubular aluminium framed children's garden chairs with a gay canvas sling seat that are much less expensive than traditional nursery chairs and can be easily transported from room to room.

The interior

Although most children consider that they have a divine right of entry into all areas of the household, they invariably regard their own room as strictly private territory—an escape area, where beloved toys can be left undisturbed, secret games can be played and where the first notions of a sense of property, personal responsibility and order start to emerge. It can therefore be a good idea to approach the design and furnishing of a child's room on the basis of consultation and team effort, rather than simply projecting your own childhood nostalgia, tastes and ideas into a scheme that will have very little meaning or significance to an opinionated three year old. Start by trying to elicit some basic information. What colours does he like? Would he prefer plain or patterned walls? Curtains or blinds? A carpet or hard floor surface? The answers may be ambiguous, impractical and well beyond your budget, but at least a picture of the room will emerge that will allow you to discuss compromise solutions and reach a degree of mutual involvement which, I believe, is essential if a child is really going to feel happy in his room.

Making use of ceilings

The nursery ceiling is the first area of the house discovered by a baby in his crib. Later, as he grows older, it becomes an inaccessible surface that seems as remote as the sky and is, at the same time, one of the most under-utilised areas in a child's room. Apart from enlivening the ceiling area with painted bands of colour or creating illusory efforts with stencil patterns, why not devise a demountable ceiling section, in the form of a central play table, suspended on ropes and operated by pulleys in much the same way as a traditional kitchen clothes rack? The lower surface can be decorated to create an interesting area of pattern and

texture in the room when pulled up to the ceiling, and the top surface will allow plenty of scope for installing a full-scale train track, toy village or zoo that need never be disturbed but is simply pulled up out of the way when not in use. As a safety precaution, however, it is important to locate the rope controls well above the reach of small children, and to make sure that the lowered table cannot swing too freely.

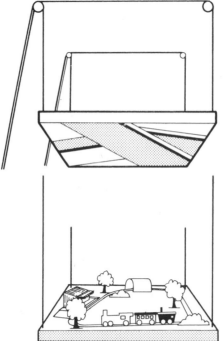

Walls

As I mentioned before, in the early months of life walls represent security and a source of constant visual stimulation to the young baby. The older child continues to be fascinated by their surface pattern and texture but, at the same time, he has an irresistible

urge to possess them, usually through elaborate drawing exercises with any tool that comes to hand—lipstick, crayons, felt pens, anything will do. It is essential to provide ample scope for such activity, first by creating pinning and scribbling surfaces around the room, from skirting level to a height of about 1 metre. This can be done in various ways, according to your budget and your ability as a competent do-it-yourselfer. Hardboard panels, for example, can be applied to the wall and painted with two or three coats of blackboard paint over a base coat of emulsion, to create a smooth chalk drawing surface. Pinboard areas can be created with sheets of cork composition—now available in colours, as well as natural brown—or chipboard panels, covered with a thin layer of sheet foam and wrapped in gaily coloured felt. Lastly, a piece of pegboard is useful for attaching assorted string bags filled with conkers, fir cones, shells and all the other treasures children enjoy finding in the great outdoors.

The treatment of the wall above these pinning/scribbling surfaces is equally important—particularly the surfaces around the cot and bunk beds. Ideally, you should choose a robust, washable wall covering such as vinyl paper or paint.

Doors

Doors, like walls, represent separation and isolation from the rest of the household to a young child, whereas later they are the cause of many a parental reprimand—'Don't bang the door', 'Don't swing on the door', and so on. When closed, they provide additional scope for wall decoration, particularly in a child's room, and if treated in a colourful, amusing way will seem less obstructive and forbidding to the lonely occupant. Built-in cupboard doors, for example, can be decorated to represent the facade of a house, the ramparts of a castle or the entrance to a cave. If you feel you are not sufficiently skilful to attempt this type of illusory design, simply outline the beading on a panelled door in a contrasting coloured paint, or apply a simple decorative stencil pattern around the door frame. It will add a new dimension to your scheme and can always be painted out to make way for pop star posters at a later date. Lastly, doors can also provide useful extra pinboard areas, particularly in a small room. You can either stick cork insulation tiles to an existing smooth surface or apply a prepared pinboard panel, consisting of chipboard covered with a thin layer of sheet foam and wrapped in felt. This will also create a good sound barrier from the rest of the household.

Floors

The floor covering in a children's play area must obviously be safe, easy to clean and maintain. There are, however, other points to consider before taking a swift decision in favour of practical vinyl or linoleum sheet. First of all, young children relate very closely to different floor surfaces in their environment. Out of doors they are fascinated by the texture and play potential of sand, grass, stones and pavements, and at home they delight in exploring the pattern of a carpet, the geometry of a parquet floor or the texture of a shaggy rug. For them the floor is a perfect play surface—somewhere to kneel down and construct a castle, organise car races or simply lie and read a book. A few blocks of expanded foam can transform a monotonous floor area into a variable exciting landscape, adding a new dimension to the leaping and jumping exercises all children enjoy, and also offering great scope for imaginative play. The blocks should be a manageable size and covered in a tough, closely woven fabric such as cotton duck or canvas. They can then be grouped together in one corner to form a rampart, a space ship or an indoor play house, and can always be used for extra seating when other children come to tea.

The floor covering itself should be equally inviting for play activities and here it is certainly worth considering a tough washable carpet that is cheap enough to be relaxed about but of sufficiently good quality to withstand the wear and tear of daily life in the play room. Ideally, I suggest you choose a hard twist design, with a small all-over pattern in a neutral colour that will not show every mark. Alternatively, you can be quite confident about installing cork or vinyl flooring. Although significantly less comfortable and warm to play on, this type of floor surface will certainly prove easier to clean and will involve comparatively little maintenance over a long period.

You only have to look at children playing on a hopscotch area on a pavement to realise how they would enjoy the chance of drawing on their own playroom floor area. This need not be as impractical as it sounds—so long as they use chalk or washable finger paint why not provide a suitable floor canvas for them? You can also create a built-in games floor yourself by using inexpensive self-adhesive tiles. Coloured tiles, for example, can be used to create a dramatic checquer board design or a gaily coloured draughts board pattern. They are easy to lay and only need mopping over with a damp cloth for day-to-day cleaning. With any hard floor surface of this kind, however, it is advisable to apply a non-slip seal polish regularly to avoid the possibility of accidents.

*Left: It would be difficult to feel isolated in this gaily painted nursery interior where the door, walls and ceilings have been integrated into an outdoor landscape.
Below: Sheets of smooth hardboard tacked on to a wooden floor can be stained or painted to create an indoor race track.*

About the house

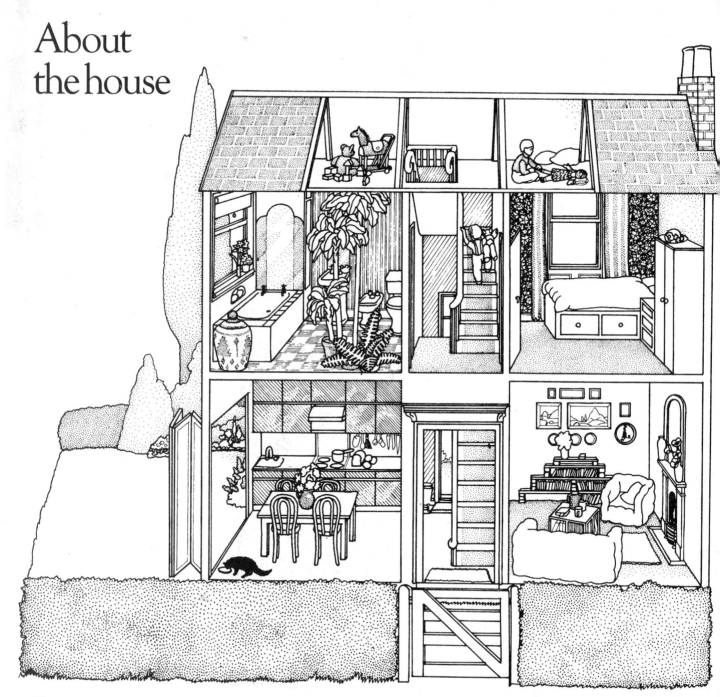

What is a house? In elevation it is simply a carcase, consisting of so many square metres of floor space—here a wall, there a door—empty, cold and lifeless until the moment it is invaded by a family. All at once, this objective machine for living is transformed into a series of precise territories—each with its own laws of entry, activity and behaviour. As adults, we have already been conditioned into observing well-defined boundaries within our domestic environment, but children are less ready to accept rules of restricted entry, particularly into areas such as a study or parents' bedroom that represent a mysterious aspect of adult life which they are not permitted to share. In the past it was easier to impose such rules, particularly in large households where children were allocated to a nursery floor and parents had their own impenetrable reserves in the form of a drawing room, library, dressing room and so on. Nowadays, pressure on living space has resulted in free-for-all rights of entry throughout the house. Although this is acceptable to many parents, it imposes a certain degree of stress on very young children who generally feel happier and more secure within certain well-defined spaces.

The importance of safety

Apart from a sense of psychological security, it is also essential that children should be physically safe in the home. Consider the accident potential of an unguarded kitchen stove, scalding water from a bathroom tap, a dimly lit flight of stairs or an open front door. It is obvious that certain areas of the house should be forbidden to unaccompanied small children, whereas they should be allowed complete freedom to enjoy the safety of the garden (if it really is safe) or play room. It follows that, from an early age, children should be taught to observe certain rules about shared areas of the house, particularly the family living room, where adult books, records, collections and hobby equipment cannot all be kept out of reach and furniture needs to be treated with respect.

Once this is achieved even the smallest household can provide a satisfactory framework for family life in which both parents and children can pursue their own activities and interests without resorting to open conflict over territorial reserves.

Later on I shall discuss the planning of shared areas of the house but, since physical safety is the most important design priority in any space occupied by children, I propose to start with the restricted territories of the hall/landing/stairs complex, the kitchen and the family bathroom.

Halls, stairs and landings

As a main circulation centre, as well as possibly a direct exit on to a busy street, the entrance hall is a particularly hazardous area in any household. First of all it must be well lit. Make sure that light fittings are fixed so that they reveal the location and height of stair treads, an internal doorstep or the angle of a sharp corner. Light switches should be positioned at a safe and accessible height for both adults and children— about 750 mm from the floor—and staircase lights should be operated by a two-way switch at both top and bottom levels. Floor surfaces should be even and non-slip and you should make certain that all stair coverings are firmly fixed and in good repair, and that there are no loose edges or joins to trip over. Mothers carrying babies or young children are particularly at risk in the house, so it is essential to make regular checks on all floor coverings for any signs of dangerous wear and tear. Later, when children no longer need to be carried, you must decide whether to install a safety gate at the top of the stairs. In my experience it is well worth taking the time to teach an active crawler how to negotiate the stairs himself (by sliding down on his front, feet first) since a safety gate often only provides a further incentive to explore the stairs and can be a considerable hazard to the unwary adult. Also, a busy mother may forget to replace the gate before rushing to answer the telephone, leaving the stairs wide open to an adventurous, but untaught, child. A safety gate is a must, however, if you possess a flight of stairs with open risers or dangerous banisters with vertical rails more than 100 mm apart. In this case, I would advise a portable, extending design of gate that can be installed at the top or bottom of the stairs, depending on where you and your child happen to be. The front door and all other doors leading into the entrance hall should be equally well protected with safety locks and handles well above the reach of toddlers. Landing windows should also have a safety locking device and, if they can be easily reached by children, I would advise the added safety precaution of a protective metal grid, fixed to the exterior window frame.

Storage in the hall

You will have to provide adequate indoor storage for coats, boots, prams, and outdoor toys and, ideally, this should be within easy reach of the entrance hall. If you are fortunate enough to possess a cloakroom or walk-in cupboard next to your entrance area, all you need to do is install enough

clothes hooks at low level for your own children's outdoor gear, as well as two or three extra coat pegs for visiting friends. Wellington boots can also be slung on low pegs if, like many designs nowadays, they have a loophole on the back, whereas hats, scarves, mittens, and school bags are best stored on open shelves, preferably within easy reach of all members of the family. I have found that even an eighteen month old child enjoys retrieving his outdoor coat and boots himself and soon learns how to put them away after an outdoor play session. Unfortunately there is no simple answer to storing unwieldy play equipment, prams and pushchairs. The best solution is to buy folding, lightweight transport equipment for your children and accept the fact that it will take up valuable floor space in your storage cupboard until outgrown and thankfully discarded. Similarly, wheeled traffic, like pedal cars and tricycles will have to be stored as neatly as possible on the floor. Even if you have enough room for them on a wide shelf, it would be a dangerous solution to the problem, since they are too heavy for a young child to lift down unaided and one day he will certainly attempt to retrieve them himself, probably with disastrous results.

Those who do not have a built-in cloakroom will either have to install a cupboard in the entrance area or make do with whatever space is available in the **cupboard under the stairs.** If it is at all possible to leave this space free, I would strongly advise you to find an alternative space for storing outdoor clothes. In my experience the cupboard under the stairs, provided that it contains no dangerous gas or electricity meters or fuses, combines all the ingredients of a perfect, ready-made play house, particularly during the winter months when children have fewer opportunities to escape to a tree house or tent in the garden.

The sloping ceilings, secret corners and curious proportions of a traditional cupboard under the stairs have infinite play possibilities for small children. My own cupboard at home has been totally transformed with shiny orange paint, a length of gaily coloured carpet and one or two posters, and is now a fully equipped mini household with its baby

bath, cooker made from an upturned carton, small-scale furniture and shopping basket filled with favourite toys. This is also where the most successful tea parties have been staged, leaving the family living area mercifully free from party debris such as discarded crisps, spilt orange squash and half-eaten chocolate biscuits.

The family bathroom

A family bathroom should be safe, practical and easy to maintain. It should also be designed to cope with the general storage of bathroom toiletries and accessories, as well as the specialised storage requirements relating to nappy changing, children's bathtime play, family first aid and so forth. As one of the most potentially dangerous areas of any house—small children have been known to drown in two or three centimetres of water and can easily scald themselves when using the more accessible taps on a bath or bidet—the bathroom should be strictly out of bounds to unaccompanied toddlers. On the other hand, a well-planned bathroom area which has the right fittings at the right height can contribute to early independence in hand-washing, teeth cleaning and toilet training and, if warm and comfortable, should be the scene for many happy bathroom sessions.

Baths in safety

A non-slip **floor surface** is essential in any bathroom area, particularly one used by children, who are expert at splashing water on the floor. Although eminently non-slip, I would never recommend a carpet for a children's bathroom. It is much better to install vinyl or plastic sealed cork tiles, which are pleasant to walk on with bare feet and will withstand frequent mopping up operations. The **bath** itself constitutes a considerable safety hazard for young children. Taps should either be mounted on the wall or set flush with the side of the bath. It is well worth having a shower spray fitting which is extremely useful for washing children's hair as well as for cleaning out a muddy bathtub. The bath should be equipped with easily accessible grab-rails, and it will certainly help if the sides are low enough for the older children to climb in and out unaided. A **rubber safety mat** should be used at all times. Young children have a tendency to lock themselves inside bathrooms and lavatories so make sure that the doors are fitted with a **two-way bolt** indicator that can be opened from the outside. Similarly, a high door handle is a good way of restricting unaccompanied entry into the bathroom.

Although a damp steamy atmosphere is unsuitable for drugs storage, the majority of bathrooms contain a **medicine cabinet** and here extra care is vital when there are young children about. The under-five age group—especially $1\frac{1}{2}$–$2\frac{1}{2}$ year olds—are the chief victims of home poisoning accidents, aspirin being the main killer. It is therefore essential to use a lockable, purpose-made cabinet that meets British Standards Institution design and safety requirements and is appropriately marked with the BS number 3922. At the same time you should observe the following basic safety procedure with regard to all medicines:

1 Never put medicines on a baby's pram when returning from the chemist. Babies have died through taking quantities of medicine left with them in this way.
2 Always give or take the exact dose of medicine prescribed—with many medicines it is dangerous to take less, or more than the doctor orders.
3 Never allow a child to dose himself even if visually supervised.
4 Never keep medicines at your bedside.
5 Keep all medicines in their original containers with labels intact.
6 Never put medicines into unlabelled containers and never mix different tablets in one container.
7 Keep medicines for internal use separate from creams and other preparations for external use.
8 Never hoard surplus medicines when illness is over or treatment has changed.
9 Dispose of medicines safely by flushing them down the lavatory or ask your chemist to destroy them for you. Never

put them in the dustbin or on the fire.

Lastly, if a poisoning accident does occur, send for the doctor immediately or take the child to your nearest hospital. Keep the container and any residue of medicine to help identify the cause of the accident and, if possible estimate the amount consumed.

Heating the bathroom

A central heating system is the safest most practical method of heating a bathroom. If this is not available, choose a wall-mounted radiant heater connected to a power point *outside* the bathroom and operated with a cord-controlled switch. The light should also be operated in this way.

Right: Step-up, potty and trainer seat from Mothercare.

Fittings and equipment

In the early years there is really no substitute for those mini lavatories and low-level hand-basins found in most primary school cloakrooms. The only way to overcome the height problem is to use a **step-up** in front of the lavatory and hand-basin. Equally, it is useful to

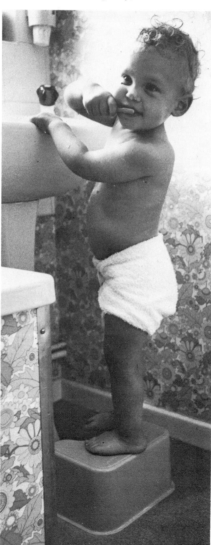

have a cistern handle positioned within easy reach of children. They will soon learn how to operate it, saving you unnecesary trips to the bathroom once they are able to use the lavatory unaided. You will, however, need one or two items of specialist nursery equipment at the earlier toilet training stage. Make sure that the **potty** you buy has a wide firm base and that the interior is easy to clean. A splash-guard which makes it suitable for both sexes and an integral hand-grip are both points to look out for when choosing a design. You will also need a **trainer seat** which reduces the size of the pan opening, making it appear less alarming to an uninitiated two year old. They are inexpensive, much easier to transport and more hygienic than a potty, so it is worth introducing one early on in toilet training.

Storage

Well-planned storage creates an efficient bathroom interior and at the same time, may well prevent a fatal accident. After-shave lotion, bath crystals, nail varnish, shampoo and foundation cream are just a few items that are generally stored in a family bathroom and which can cause poisoning if consumed by children. It is essential to provide suitable storage for general accessories, as well as for the specialist equipment needed in the daily nappy/toilet training routines. Begin by making an itemised list starting with towels, toothpaste, bath brush, nail brush, and not forgetting those dangerous chemical cleaners that usually end up on the bathroom shelf or tucked under the basin. Some things are best hung on hooks or, in the case of toothbrushes and mugs, can be fitted into purpose-designed wall brackets. Cleaning products should be concealed in a small, ventilated cupboard above child reach and favourite bath toys should be easily accessible from the bath— preferably arranged on an adjacent shelf. If you have space, it is a good idea to install a wide, laminate-topped vanitory unit, with lockable drawers for cosmetics and toiletries and space below for one or two mobile storage boxes fitted with lift-off cork lids. These can be used for stowing dirty linen and housing bulky items such as a bucket, trainer seat or potty and will also double up as useful low-level stools at bathtime.

A small family bathroom

There can be very few family bathrooms smaller than our own 2.2 m × 1.7 m interior, and yet it works perfectly well, even with two under-fives in the home. During the early years, I put a strong board over the bath top. Covered with a gaily printed PVC fabric, it provided an excellent nappy changing surface and was large enough to take a baby bath on top, together with a small basket for toiletries. If you can use a sewing machine, it is also a good idea to attach a series of pockets to the front edge of the board for storing toiletries, pins and so on. The 530 mm wide basin is recessed in a corner and an overhead cupboard provides safe, inaccessible storage for bathroom toiletries, cleaning equipment etc. The bath has a 200 mm wide shelf on one side for storing bathtime toys and there is just enough floor space alongside for a pedestal stool and a nappy bucket under the basin. Lastly, the plastic-sealed cork floor and white tiled walls are both easy to clean and maintain, and the high door handle successfully prevents the entry of anyone under three years old.

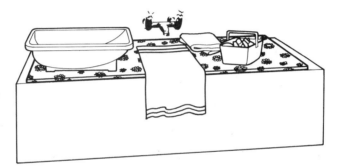

Planning a family kitchen

As a power house of potentially dangerous machines and the home of sharp utensils and poisonous cleaning agents, the family kitchen should be strictly 'forbidden territory' to unaccompanied small children. On the other hand, the average domestic kitchen is filled with the originals of the expensive model learning equipment that you can now find in playgroups and nursery schools, so once you have investigated all the safety factors and planned the space in terms of visual supervision, ease of maintenance and work pattern, it can become a successful play area, as well as a practical food preparation centre, home laundry and family eating/meeting place.

How you plan your family kitchen area is very much a question of the space available and how much you want to spend. Most mothers would agree, however, that a kitchen-cum-family room is an excellent solution to the problem of coping with under-fives while pursuing the daily cooking and household chores. It allows you to keep an eye on them playing while you work since, for the majority of their waking hours, you will need to be in the kitchen. For detailed advice and information on all kitchen design problems, you should see the companion volume in this series, 'Planning Your Kitchen' by José and Michael Manser. For the purposes of this book, however, I will point out some of the most important design considerations in equipping a kitchen/living area where there are children in the house.

Appliances

A determined climber will reach even the highest controls on a **cooker**, so this need not be an over-riding consideration when it comes to choosing one. What you should consider carefully, though, is where you position the cooker in your kitchen. There is a greater risk of fire, for example, if it is installed under a window where draughts can fan flames or blow out burners and curtains can quickly catch fire. There is also danger in leaning over hot-plates and burners to open or clean a window. To make work easier, the cooker should stand away from corners and have related work surfaces and storage alongside. Here, split-level designs offer considerable advantages over floor-standing models, since hot plates or burners can be recessed into work tops at a convenient height and out of the reach of very small children.

The disappearance of the traditional cold larder in the modern kitchen has resulted in a demand for larger **refrigerators** to store foods that merely need cool conditions, not freezing temperatures. This particularly applies to young family households where it is necessary to store prepared feeding bottles, opened jars of baby food, and extra quantities of fresh fruit and vegetables, in a cold place. It is a good idea to invest in the largest refrigerator you can afford and that you have room for—preferably with a large frozen food storage compartment. This can then be stocked with supplies of the frozen foods that most children adore, such as fish fingers, sausages, frozen peas, sweet corn, ice cream and so forth, so that you need not shop every day or be caught out when a tribe of unexpected small visitors turns up for a meal.

The average daily time spent at the sink without a **dishwasher** is 68 minutes, whereas an automatic machine will wash, rinse and dry a full load of dishes in 15 to 90 minutes depending on its size and design. The loading, setting of controls and unloading, takes about three minutes in all, so there are some substantial reasons for investing in a dishwasher, particularly for a young family. When it comes to choosing a model, remember that capacity is usually measured by the number of place settings. The number varies from between six and twelve, but I would advise buying the largest you can afford and have space for. Most designs nowadays are front loading and can therefore be installed under a work top alongside the sink area, but remember that drop-down doors need at least 550 mm clearance space in front of them and all machines need a little extra space for pipe-work when plumbed in. Lastly, make sure that the one you buy has been approved by the British Electro-technical Approvals Board and is appropriately marked with the blue and yellow BEAB symbol.

An automatic **washing machine** is an essential item of domestic equipment for any mother and it is worth going without a lot of other things to acquire this right from the start. A single tub machine is obviously the best solution for a shared kitchen/family room where laundry space is often at a premium. Alternatively, if you can possibly find the space for a self-contained laundry room on the ground floor, it will certainly prove worth the extra expense, since washing and drying machines, ironing boards and irons are all notoriously dangerous items of equipment for small children, and you will find it much more convenient to carry out the daily laundry routine away from the food preparation area. Although not essential, a **tumble drier** is a valuable item of home laundry equipment—particularly during the cold, wet winter months when it is difficult to dry things inside a small home. Nowadays, many models can be stacked on top of companion, or existing washing machines so as to take up less floor space in a small kitchen or laundry room.

Although a shrewd choice of garments and easy-care fabrics will greatly reduce the task of ironing, no efficient home laundry is complete without a good, up-to-date **iron.** Both steam and dry irons are now lighter in weight and some steam irons have special spraying attachments which are invaluable for the home dress-maker. Most designs are marked with the now universally recognised Home Laundry Consultative Council scale of iron heats which, like the washing-code, should avoid costly accidents to the family wardrobe. Lastly, make sure that your **ironing board** is stable, has a safe iron rest and a flex support to prevent tangling and the possibility of accidents whilst in use.

Play in the kitchen
A sink filled with water and a varied supply of pouring utensils; a pair of measuring scales and a heap of raisins; a lump of pastry and a rolling pin—these are just a few ways of keeping a toddler safely and happily occupied in the kitchen while you prepare a meal. Of course there will be a mess, but a peaceful half-hour is well worth the trouble of cleaning up afterwards.

Water
Playing at the sink is an all-time favourite with under-fives and an excellent way of keeping a young child busy while you labour over a hot stove. Stand him on a high chair with the tray in position so that he feels safe and can sit down when he wants to. Make sure that he is adequately protected with a plastic apron and put an old towel down on the floor—there is no way of preventing the occasional spill, intentional or otherwise. Add a small amount of washing-up liquid to the water and provide plenty of plastic containers, wooden utensils, a funnel, bottle brush and, best of all, a short length of plastic tubing. He will soon master the art of pouring and siphoning water, while acquiring coordination and knowledge of what floats, sinks or breaks.

Elementary cooking
Pastry-making, baking and all other cooking pursuits that involve the weighing, measuring and stirring of ingredients, can be shared activities and are always enjoyed by young children. Again there will be a mess to clear up, but it is better than having to stop the job in order to break up a quarrel, repair a broken toy or look for a lost one. It is also an excellent introduction to junior cookery. By the time a child is three years old he will be able to carry out simple verbal instructions and at four he should be able to follow an illustrated recipe sheet, under visual supervision.

A nature table
It is a good idea to set aside a low-level shelf or work surface for arranging and displaying all the strange objects that children delight in finding out of doors. Otherwise your kitchen will become a depository for conkers, flowers, dead leaves, stones, fir cones and all the other favourite discoveries. At the same time,

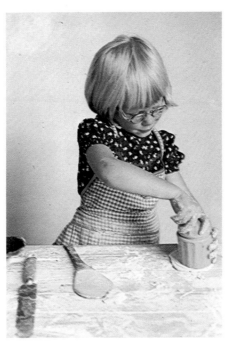

you can use the surface for the family fish tank, bird or gerbil cage, as well as for growing bulbs, mustard and cress or even a miniature indoor rock garden. Once the children have seen growing experiments of this kind, they will quickly start others themselves, leaving the remaining kitchen work tops free for your own cooking activities.

Play materials

The kitchen is plentifully supplied with play materials that are safe, easy to use and produce quick and effective results when teamed with a pot of home-made flour and water paste. Large sheets of newspaper, for example, are cheaper than expensive art paper for finger painting and potato printing. Discarded kitchen roll centres, foil dishes, egg boxes, milk cartons, paper plates and doilies provide excellent material for puppet-making. Dry foods, such as lentils, cornflakes and pasta of all kinds add colour and texture to a collage, and all children love making their own modelling dough with flour, salt, food colouring and water. It is worth establishing a 'Making Things' box or carrier bag in the kitchen so that useful materials are not inadvertently thrown away and the children know where to retrieve them themselves.

Safety

One only has to scan a page of home accident statistics to understand how essential it is to provide a safe area in which you can work and your children can play. According to a recent ROSPA report, twenty people die each day from accidents in the home in Great Britain, and every year more than $1\frac{1}{2}$ million people are treated in hospital for accidents of this kind. The ROSPA statistics also show that home accidents fall into five main categories—poisoning, burns, scalds, falls, and suffocation— and many of these are directly related to the kitchen area. You should therefore start by checking your kitchen against the following accident list:

Poisoning

There are two kinds of domestic poison accidents:
1 Inhalation of poisonous gases and vapours.
2 Swallowing poisonous liquids and solids.

Prevention 1: Keep gas appliances in good repair, have them checked regularly for blocked flues and vents, and make sure that the room is adequately ventilated. Only buy British Gas approved appliances. Try to prevent liquids from boiling over and, if this does occur, check that the pilot light is working afterwards. Turn off the mains supply when leaving the house for more than 24 hours and always turn off the tap before putting money in prepayment meters.

Prevention 2: Always keep chemical cleaners and all poisonous substances in a locked cupboard, out of reach of small children, remembering that even a two year old standing on a chair can reach well over a metre. Here is a list of substances which can cause poisoning and which are likely to be found in and around the kitchen area: adhesives, air freshener blocks, ammonia, bleach, carpet cleaner, caustic soda, clothing dye, detergent, disinfectant, dry-cleaning liquids, fertilizer liquids, fire lighters, French polish, glue, ink remover, marking ink, insecticide, match heads, metal polish, moth balls, oven cleaner, paint, paint brush restorer, paint stripper, paraffin, scouring powder, shoe polish, silver polish, suede dye, toilet cleaner, turpentine, washing powder, washing-up liquid, window cleaner.

Burns

Burning accidents are most likely to occur during the winter months when fires of all kinds are in frequent use. But you should be vigilant all the time, particularly where matches, flammable liquids and hot appliances are concerned. Prevention: Use flame resistant fabrics wherever possible and certainly for kitchen curtains. Store matches well out of the reach of children. Never leave a fire unguarded—fire and heat provide an early learning experience for children, so teach them from the start that it hurts. This also applies to hot pans, ovens and hot-plates. Never leave clothes to air near an unguarded heat source. Keep all flammable fluids in metal containers well out of the way of small children.

Scalds

Small children and tired housewives are the chief victims of domestic scalding accidents which tend to occur mainly in kitchen and bathroom areas. Prevention: Keep children out of the cooking area when hot liquids are prepared and used. Turn pan handles and kettle spouts away from the front of the cooker out of a child's reach. It is best to forget tablecloths altogether during the early years since toddlers are adept at pulling them off—frequently with disastrous results. Keep the flex of electrical hand appliances such as kettles, irons and mixers hooked up away from small children. Put cold water in the sink first, adding hot water

to reach the required temperature. Although in principle it is a good idea to install a pan guard on the cooker, recent statistics have shown that they can cause as many accidents as they prevent. Children have been known to pull a pan into the guard causing scalds that would have been avoided if the pan had fallen away from the body onto the floor. Adults too can forget that there is a two-fold action in removing a hot pan from a stove fitted with a guard rail and the result is an avoidable scalding accident. Nevertheless, there are many mothers who swear by them, so you must make the decision yourself.

Falls

Anyone can fall over, but mothers and children are particularly prone to this type of accident, which is even more dangerous in a kitchen area where there are hot liquids, hot pans and dishes in constant use. Prevention: All floor coverings must be in good repair and hard floors should have a non-slip surface free from polish build-up. Try to avoid using chairs to reach up to high cupboards—household steps are, after all, designed for the job. Always wipe up floor spills immediately. If you wait till you have finished cooking or serving a meal it will probably be too late. Lastly, try to keep toys off the kitchen floor.

Suffocation

Although many polythene bags nowadays carry a warning, it is essential to remove bags immediately and store them well away from small children. Always remove the door or lid of a discarded cooker, refrigerator or trunk and ask your local authority special disposal service to take away such potentially dangerous refuse as soon as possible.

Other dangers

Other accidents cause a certain number of deaths each year and a larger proportion of avoidable serious or minor injuries. For example, careless use of appliances, sharp kitchen utensils, sewing equipment and household tools can cause injury, particularly where young children are concerned. Prevention: Never allow small children to carry or play with breakable crockery or glass, cutlery, jagged tins, razor blades, scissors and so on. Wrap breakages in plenty of newspaper. Sweep rather than pick up the broken pieces. Never store heavy items on high shelves or attempt to stop a spin dryer or electric wringer by hand—it will certainly not save time, and you or your child may end up with broken fingers.

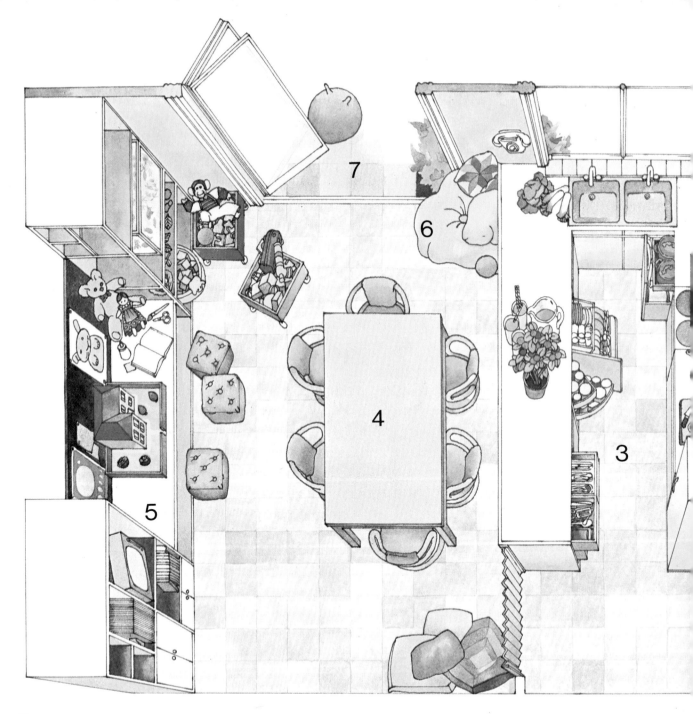

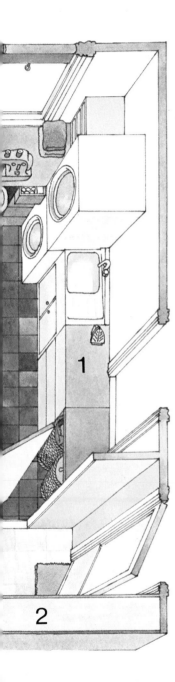

A kitchen scheme

In this kitchen/family room scheme, the design emphasis is on a small, well-organised kitchen work station—a relaxed, child-orientated living/play space and an informal adults' dining/entertaining area.

1 The self-contained laundry unit is equipped with a stacking automatic washing machine and tumble drier, allowing enough space for a small sewing area, complete with sewing machine, adjacent ironing facilities and a lockable drawer storage unit for potentially dangerous sewing accessories. The laundry room also has a sink for hand-washing small or delicate garments and a dirty clothes basket recessed under the work-top.

2 The floor-to-ceiling cupboard unit provides easily accessible storage alongside the back door for boots, coats, and outdoor toys. The high-level cupboards are useful for storing out-of-season gear, such as tennis rackets, an inflatable paddling pool, or buckets and spades.

3 The kitchen area has a dishwasher, a large fridge and a floor-standing cooker, fitted with a ducted hood—essential in any dual purpose kitchen area. The storage units alongside the living area are equipped with a safety lip and are used for china, glass, cutlery and all the other things you need near an eating area. The backs of the units provide pinning and scribbling space for younger members of the family, who are kept out of danger by an extending safety gate, that can easily be removed when outgrown.

4 The sturdy laminate-topped dining table—suitable for model-making and homework activities later on—can be disguised with a cloth for adult evening parties.

5 The adjustable open-shelving system is designed to house your children's things where they can reach them—and yours where they can't. Adult books, records, radio/television are therefore all accommodated on high shelves. The central low-level work bench has some storage space next to it for construction kits, puzzles, or doll's house furniture whereas racing cars, building bricks and other toys that are best played with on the floor, are stowed in mobile toy boxes and shallow plastics washing-up bowls. The remaining lower shelf space is allocated to a nature table and family pet station.

6 Sturdy floor cushions and a sack chair provide adequate seating and avoid constant reprimands for jumping on furniture.

7 The outdoor terraced area is covered with a conservatory-style glass roof, providing a warm, dry pram park or play space, that can be watched over from the kitchen and avoids the inevitable muddy foot-marks from children running in and out from the garden.

How to escape

All parents need their own escape routes from family—either in the form of a bedroom, home-office, sitting room or study, depending on the size and scope of the house. Children need not be excluded from such areas altogether, but they should clearly understand that entry is by invitation only and that a closed door indicates a parental bid for peace and quiet.

The parents' bedroom

This is likely to be the only possible refuge in a small home, so it should be designed to provide for evening relaxation as well as for sleeping, clothes storage and the inevitable early morning invasion of the under-fives. Start by re-thinking your existing space in terms of its potential as a dual-purpose bedroom/sitting area. Simple alterations, such as blocking up a redundant fireplace, re-hanging a door or inserting full height storage in an awkward corner recess, need not cost a lot of money and you will be surprised how much space they gain in a small room. At the same time, consider your existing furniture and work out the best possible arrangement, with cut-out representations on a scale plan, remembering that ideally you need a minimum of 700 mm on either side and at the foot of the bed for general circulation and bed-making. To avoid draughts, the bedhead should not be placed either beneath the window or in a direct line between the window and door. You may on the other hand decide to dispense with a conventional bed altogether, preferring a folding bed/storage unit in order to create more space for a daytime work station, sewing area or home office.

Storage

It is impossible to have a relaxing sitting area or efficient work station if there are clothes on the floor and cosmetics on top of the typewriter, so adequate storage is essential in a dual-purpose bedroom interior. The best way to tackle the problem is to draw up a list of storage requirements related to each activity, so that you can work out just how much storage you will need in the room right from the start. Here is a guide, starting with the basic activities of sleeping, bed-making and dressing that are common to all bedroom areas.

Activity	Storage equipment
Sleep	Bedside storage for nightwear water decanter and glass radio alarm clock books
Bed-making	Deep drawer storage for sheets, pillowcases blankets or duvet
Dressing	Hanging storage for clothes drawer storage for folded garments rack for shoes shallow drawers for small accessories deep drawer storage for out-of-season clothes

Specialised storage

Parents' working area: A pedestal desk with drawer space for correspondence, stationery and writing materials should meet the basic storage requirements of a working area in the bedroom. But in order to ensure that the main work surface is free for a variety of activities, from sewing to concentrated study, you will need additional storage provision alongside for bulky equipment, such as a typewriter or sewing machine; adjacent shelves for large reference books, telephone directories and catalogues, as well as specialised storage for sewing equipment, stray paper patterns, correspondence files and so on. In my own bedroom working area, I have solved the problem with a wall pocket storage unit in white moulded plastics which takes small stationery and sewing accessories, includes a clipboard section for invitations and bills, as well as pocket space for catalogues, address book and other reference material—all above child level and yet within easy reach of my working surface. The sewing machine and typewriter are stored in the base of a nearby floor-to-ceiling cupboard unit fitted with child-proof sliding doors and a tiered filing tray copes with day-to-day correspondence.

Hobby area

Specialised storage for hobby activities can range from a housing unit for a tape recorder to a lockable store for photographic developing liquids, so it is essential to take all interests into account when planning your storage system. In principle, you will need to provide plenty of accessible shelving for books and study materials alongside the working area; pinboard space is valuable for charts, photographs and bull-dog clipped material; locker storage beneath the bed is useful for stowing bulky equipment, musical instruments, magazines or painting materials and high-level cupboards can cope with seasonal games and hobby equipment.

Lastly, it is a good idea to allow a small amount of storage space for a few favourite children's books and one or two quiet games that can be played in the mornings—otherwise your tidy bedside storage unit will soon be submerged with children's clutter. If you have room for a small toy box at the foot of the bed, this is a good solution since they will be able to retrieve their possessions themselves—and, hopefully, put them away again. Alternatively, set aside a drawer under the bed, or a low level shelf nearby.

Lighting

A general diffused light fitting controlled by a switch near the door is essential in a bedroom area which is frequently entered in the dark. It should be teamed with a wall-mounted reading light by the bed, as well as additional directional lighting for other specialised activities where needed. For example, a wall-mounted spotlight, an adjustable table lamp or angled light fitting with a clamp base are three practical solutions to lighting a working area. A strategically placed adjustable fitting also does the job of several fixed fittings and is particularly useful for lighting a multi-purpose work station.

Walls and floors

Although patterned wallpapers are a traditional bedroom wall covering, I would think carefully before buying a vivid geometric or busy flower design. Remember that you may have to stare at it for hours from a sick bed, whereas a plain, neutral coloured surface is less tiring on the eye and is more suitable for a dual-purpose interior. A vinyl hessian paper is a good compromise, since the textured surface immediately creates a general feeling of quiet warmth in the room and it is also very practical —particularly behind the bed and around a washbasin area. Alternatively, eggshell or vinyl paint is cheap and easy to renew, but again I would suggest that you choose a light neutral colour which will contrast well with the various patterns and textures created by books, desk accessories and other paraphernalia.

A fitted carpet is a good solution to covering a bedroom floor if you can afford it. It is pleasant to walk on with bare feet and, compared with other rooms in the house, it will not have to stand up to a lot of hard wear and tear. It will also create an immediate sense of warmth and comfort—essential in any parental relaxation area.

Out of doors

Transport

The equipment you need for transporting your children depends on their age and your own methods and means of transport. For example, if you live within walking distance of a shopping centre you will need a pram, for the first year or so, that is large enough to accommodate a baby as well as the daily shopping load. Alternatively, if you have to drive to a shopping centre you will need a carry-cot, secured on the back seat with safety straps, together with a folding transporter for wheeling your baby around when you get there.

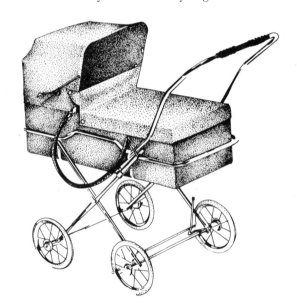

When it comes to choosing a suitable **pram** there are several important points to consider. Firstly there is the question of indoor storage. Few houses nowadays have space for the coach-built designs favoured by traditionalists. In any case you may be living in a block of flats with little or no ground-floor storage, so probably, the wisest, and incidentally most economical, decision is to buy a dual-purpose design that incorporates a sturdy carry-cot on a folding transporter base. Alternatively, you can buy a convertible pram/pushchair that is suitable for the youngest baby and, at the same time, can be easily converted into a pushchair at a later date.

When shopping for a pram remember the following points:

1 Is the handle correctly positioned? If it is too high the pram may tip up while you are pushing. If too low, you will return home with a back ache.

2 Make sure that you can handle the pram safely and comfortably, particularly when negotiating steps and kerb stones.

3 Make sure that you can see over the hood when it is up.

4 Is there a strong, well attached harness fastening? Babies have been known to swallow loose screws and fittings of this kind.

5 Is there enough space for shopping and/or a baby's accessory bag when out for the day? The British Standard for prams covers quality of construction and, at the same time, provides for a high standard of safety and durability. Points to look out for include brakes on at least two wheels, positioned well out of reach of the child; a firm interior lining to prevent suffocation; and an inside depth of at least 190 mm. These conditions apply to both folding and rigid body prams and you should certainly make sure that the design you buy carries a kitemark label and is marked with the BS number 4139.

A closely-fitting **pram net** is essential if your baby is to be left to sleep

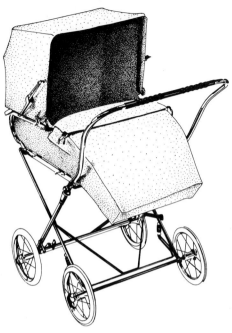

unattended out of doors. The fine-mesh variety will protect him from cats as well as stinging insects and flies, and he will not entangle his fingers in the netting.

A lightweight folding **pushchair** is essential for transporting a toddler and there are some excellent collapsible designs available which can be folded and slung over your arm when negotiating stairs and escalators. These very light designs often do not have any space for your shopping though, so if you do not use a car you may have to buy a more traditional design with a wire carrying basket at the back. There has recently been concern over accidents to children trapping themselves in folding pushchairs, so try to keep the chair stored away when not in use and look out for the British Standard BS 4792. Whatever type you choose you will certainly need an additional rain protector, which can double up for use

on a pram seat, and make sure that your child is always warmly wrapped up, since pushchairs offer very little protection against cold weather.

The new-style lightweight pushchairs have, to a certain extent, eliminated the need for a **baby carrier**, since rubber shock absorbers and a specially designed suspension make it possible to negotiate even the roughest terrains quite easily. On the other hand, a carrier leaves you with both hands free and is often more suitable for crowded shopping expeditions, long country walks, picnics and so forth. If possible, you should select a cantilevered frame design that transfers the baby's weight from your shoulders to your hips and avoids the painful neck and shoulder aches that can occur with other designs. Other points to look for are an adjustable canvas seat to allow for growth up to about two years, storage space for a bottle or nappies and a restraint strap that holds the child securely and yet allows plenty of freedom of movement.

Road drill

Even the most experienced pedestrians need to take extra care when pushing a pram, particularly in the early weeks when it is easy to forget the following basic safety procedure:

1 When crossing the road do not push the pram into the road ahead of you—pull it behind you. Never attempt to cross the road from between parked vehicles and always use a pedestrian crossing.

2 Never overload a pram with shopping.

3 When parking the pram always make sure that the brake is on securely—even if you are only leaving it for a few seconds.

4 If it is not possible to take the pram into a shop and you cannot watch your baby from inside *always* carry him in with you.

Safety in cars

Choosing a suitable family car is much more hazardous than selecting a baby transporter, since although most modern designs incorporate some child safety requirements, they lack others. Here are some points to check on:

1 Make sure that the car you buy is equipped with adequate child-proof safety locks.

2 Are there safety belts fitted in the back for children who have outgrown a special baby seat?

3 Is the boot large enough to transport a pram and all the baby equipment needed for an overnight stay? If not you will probably have to use a roof rack.

4 Is the upholstery washable? Always choose vinyl rather than a more opulent stretch fabric.

5 Can the hand-brake be released by a young child left unattended in the car?

It is essential for all young children to be strapped securely when travelling and as soon as your baby can sit up, you will have to install a special **safety seat** in the back of the car. This must be a BSI approved design with a harness that not only secures the seat to the car, but also keeps the child in the seat. (Never use an ordinary chair hooked over the back of the front seat).

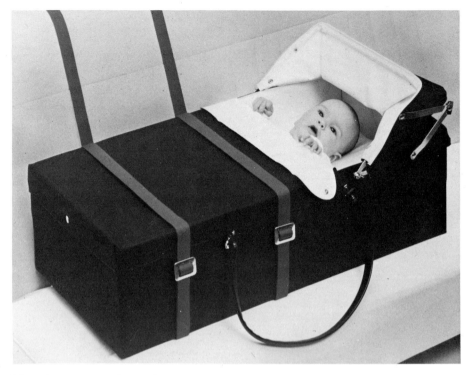

Nowadays, you can buy safety seats equipped with a harness that doubles as a child's safety belt later on.

Keeping them happy

When it comes to long car journeys with young children it is invariably better to arrive than travel. Here are some useful tips, however, which should make life easier for both parents and children:

1 Take disposable nappies and an extra plastics bag for soiled nappies and tissues.

2 Carry a waterproof bag containing a moist flannel for wiping sticky fingers.

3 Take a warm rug and a soft pillow to encourage toddlers to sleep en route.

4 A flask of juice and some food will be welcome. Make a rule when it comes to quantities—one slice of apple when we next see a church/gasometer/bridge and so forth.

Above: A restraint such as this one by Mothercare will keep a carry-cot firmly on the car seat and is easily removed when not in use.

Right: For children from about one to five, this KL Jeenay safety seat can be fitted to any car. It can be removed quickly and easily and its detachable harness can be worn on its own by older children up to about twelve.

Gardens

When it comes to planning and equipping a garden for young children, the first question to consider is how long you plan to stay in your present home. This may be unanswerable, but at least you should know whether it will be a long-term stay or simply a matter of one or two years. If it is for some time, it may be worth investing in some substantial play equipment—the sort that needs to be firmly cemented in the ground and is therefore difficult to move on to another garden. Alternatively, if you are considering a short stay, it is a good idea to buy demountable equipment that is easy to move about and can always be handed on to another family when outgrown.

The second point to consider is the sort of garden you want. You must choose between an all-out adventure playground or a child-adapted adult garden with a play enclosure sited well away from precious plants and shrubs. Inevitably, space will dictate some decisions, but ask any child what sort of garden *he* would like and the priorities will almost certainly be a smooth paved area for wheeled traffic, an area of grass for playing ball games, a pile of sand or earth for digging activities, and at least one climbable tree.

On the whole, I would advise against buying too much specialist play equipment. Swings, slides and see-saws are all extremely expensive, and freely available in municipal parks, whereas an improvised **swing,** consisting of a length of strong rope and a rubber car tyre firmly looped over a branch, will provide many hours of active play, for very little cost.

Sand and Water

All young children love playing with sand so a small **sand-pit** is a very worthwhile investment. A word of warning, however, for owners of small gardens.

Site the sand-pit as far as possible from your back door, otherwise you will spend hours sweeping up sand around the house. Although there are several purpose-made designs on the market costing around £20, a sand-pit need not be an expensive item of play equipment. Four strong planks of wood secured by angled steel clips will provide a perfectly adequate, self-draining enclosure for a heap of silver sand. (I would advise against builders' sand which tends to stain hands and clothing and, although cheaper, will not prove a worthwhile saving). In addition, you will need at least three or four buckets and spades in order to have some spare equipment for visiting children, and it is also a good idea to provide an assortment of discarded kitchen utensils. For example, a sieve, yoghurt cartons, wooden spoons, jelly moulds, and plastics containers will greatly increase the play potential of your sand-pit. Lastly, you will need a strong, waterproof cover over the sand-pit to deter cats and dogs and prevent the sand from becoming water-logged after heavy rain.

Parents should be wary of installing any permanent **water play** garden equipment, such as a paddling pool or pond—at least in the early years, when it is virtually impossible to supervise children at all times out of doors. A plastics inflatable pool, however, is a good and cheap way to provide for safe water play activities in the summer months. They are quick to assemble, fill and remove at the end of a play session, so there is no temptation to leave an unguarded pool out of doors. Alternatively, if you have a tapped water supply out in the garden—all you need is a length of hose. All children love watering plants, as well as themselves, and a lot of fun can be had for very little money or effort. Lastly, a bucket filled with water is quite adequate for making a good supply of mud pies, or irrigating a patch of earth,

Commando net (above), Variplay house and slide (top right) and child's hammock (below right) from ESA Creative Learning Limited.

and should not consitute a safety hazard if play is temporarily unsupervised.

Climbing
As the price of raw materials continues to rise so, unfortunately, does the cost of wooden climbing frames. A climbing frame, however, is an excellent investment for a young family and, if it is possible to persuade a group of friends and relatives to contribute towards the initial cost, it will certainly prove one of the longest-lasting items of play equipment you can buy. The most successful designs incorporate two movable platforms, slung at different heights, an entrance door into a ground floor play house and, if you can afford it, it is well worth paying for an additional slide.

Swinging
A monkey swing is a cheap alternative to the conventional garden frame swing, and, although not suitable for very young children, it will provide hours of amusement from the age of four upwards. Similarly, if you have a suitable tree in the garden, a rope ladder, a strong hemp climbing rope or cord hammock are all fairly inexpensive items of play equipment and are very easy to store when not in use.

It is always worth paying extra for garden play equipment—particularly when it comes to buying a wheel barrow, sand shovel, or garden tools. In any imitative play activities such as digging, sweeping up leaves or planting bulbs, children want their equipment to resemble adult tools as closely as possible, so in most cases it is better to buy the real thing rather than a lightweight toy equivalent. Small-scale trowels and hand forks are available at garden equipment shops and you can always trim the handle of a hoe or garden broom down to size.

Toys and parties

Toys

I always remember a leading toy manufacturer's response to my question 'What's new in toys this year?'. 'Only the children are new,' he replied. It is *children* who interpret, cherish, despise or reject the toys that are available on the market today, so the most important rule when shopping for any new toy is to know your child. Each one is an individual with his or her own likes and dislikes, aptitudes and skills and it is therefore essential to appeal to an individual rather than merely to an age group, when making your selection. The next consideration is safety. There is no such thing as a safe toy if it is in the wrong hands. Consider, for example, a sturdy wooden threading toy, consisting of large wooden beads painted in non-toxic paint and mounted on a wooden stand. A perfectly safe, instructive toy in the hands of an eager-to-learn two year old, but to a six-month old the wooden stand is a dangerous weapon that can easily be poked in the eyes or thrust down the throat. It is therefore essential to consider the age and skills of any child before handing over a new plaything. The British Standard Code of Safety Requirements for Children's Toys and Playthings provides for a high standard of safety and durability and you should make sure that any toy you buy complies with its rulings. The British Standards Institution, for example, stipulates that all materials used in soft toys should be non-inflammable; fillings must be clean and harmless; and eyes and limbs must be securely attached. In clockwork toys moving parts must be totally enclosed and there should be no exposed metal

Left: Young children can learn how to use fingers and thumbs by playing with specially designed toys such as this 'Flip Fingers' toy made by Kiddicraft.

edges. Folding doll's prams must have safety stops and so on. All toys that comply with British Standards Institution recommendations are indicated by the number BS 3443, so check on this before you buy.

0–18 months

Recent research into infant development has revealed that the early years are vitally important in determining the standard a child is likely to reach within the range of his inherited capabilities. You should, therefore, never underestimate a young child's ability to learn and profit from play activities of all kinds. Babies learn through their senses, so in the early months it is important to create as many new learning experiences as possible by providing plenty of things to see and touch, feel and hear. **Rattles,** for example, can stimulate several senses at the same time if they are well-designed and made of attractive, tactile material. Natural beech cage rattles are an excellent choice. They are light, easy to grasp in tiny fingers, smooth and pleasant to touch and, more important still, perfectly safe and hygienic. On the whole, I would advise against buying cheap plastics ball rattles, which break easily, and felt headed stick rattles, which although attractive to look at, do not stand up to frequent sucking and are, in my opinion, unsafe for a very young baby. **Mobiles** not only help a baby to learn to focus his eyes, they encourage him to observe movement and colour and, if correctly placed above the cot, can be an endless source of visual stimulation. Here there are no rules, but I would advise you to look outside the toy shop circuit for an alternative to the conventional nursery designs. Oriental shell mobiles, for example, provide sound as well as movement. On the other hand, if you have the time you can always make up your own design from an assortment of gaily

coloured beads, key rings, paper flowers, small toys or even baby accessories, such as a colourful shoe, hairbrush or mittens.

As soon as a baby can sit up he will try to crawl and explore his little world. At the same time, his control of hand and arm movements quickly increases so this is the moment to introduce simple **fitting, nesting and building toys,** as well as colourful objects of all kinds, which can be placed a short distance away to encourage exploration by reaching out, rolling over and crawling. You can buy excellent fitting and building toys, ranging from sturdy wooden tunnel pegs and bricks to nesting plastics beakers and sets of gaily coloured vinyl shapes for grasping, chewing and squeezing. Do not forget, however that a good plaything demands something of the child and the child demands something of it, so you need not restrict yourself to the shelves of your local toy shop. A gleaming aluminium saucepan, stacking plastics

cups, or a colourful bathroom sponge are just a few of the items that can be found around the house which will provide plenty of creative play potential for no extra cost. This is also the time when a child will start to establish a long-lasting relationship with one or other of his possessions—a soft teddy bear, a cot blanket, rag doll or, better still, a muslin nappy which can be easily washed or substituted on an outing. Later it will probably develop into a constant companion, a symbol of permanence, safety and continuity—so be prepared, and do not discourage your child from taking a cherished possession about with him if he needs it, however dirty or disreputable it may become. Finally, as soon as a child learns to walk, he will want to develop his new-found skill by pushing a vehicle or pulling a wheeled toy. **Pull-along toys** and **baby walkers** should be stable and lightweight, whereas a wheeled **cart, truck** or **pram** should be tough enough for use out of doors, as well as deep enough to transport a host of treasured belongings.

Left: A simple beech rattle inserted with a tinkling bell can stimulate the senses of touch and sound from a very early age. It is obviously still enjoyed by this lively six-month old.

Above: A ring of brightly coloured plastic beads can be placed just out of reach to encourage early experiments in crawling, as well as observation of colour and sound.

Top left: Small children are often impressed by large-scale toys.
Middle and bottom left: Basic materials such as sand and water offer great scope for group play at any age while finger painting provides an early opportunity to experiment with colour and pattern in a direct way. Above: Playing shop is a favourite imitative play activity that can be as absorbing for the individual as for the group.

18 months–3 years

At 18 months a child may know a dozen or so words and by the time he is three he will know several hundred. He enjoys scribbling with crayons, posting objects through holes, playing with sand and water, climbing on furniture and generally exploring his immediate world, with a delight and fascination that should always be encouraged and never suppressed. This is the time to distract him from turning your home into an indoor adventure playground, with play equipment that will exploit his new-found skills both safely and creatively.

First of all, language development can be encouraged by almost any plaything, from well-illustrated books to simple jigsaw puzzles. **Picture tray puzzles** are ideal for this age group. The pieces are easy to take out and replace and stories can be developed around the illustrations. Equally, **picture puzzles** encourage observation of shape and size, which will later lead to learning letters and numbers, and they can provide a valuable early learning experience. It is important for all illustrative material at this stage to be easily identifiable and relate closely to the child and his world, for this is when he starts to work

out and connect up his immediate surroundings. Pictures should be accurate and depict real-life situations. Imitative play equipment, such as small-scale carpet sweepers, doll's prams, kitchen utensils and gardening tools, should be long-lasting and strong and must function properly in order to build up security, confidence and an understanding of how things work. With increasing movement and muscular dexterity a child of this age will also enjoy **activity toys** such as a tough wheeled truck or tricycle, which can be propelled at speed around the house and garden. A safe rocking seat or horse, will give great pleasure and enjoyment and will increase confidence in movement.

At this stage too, early imaginative play can be stimulated by **constructional toys** of all kinds. A sack of play bricks, a set of wooden connecting rods or plastics building blocks can quickly be transformed by a

Above left: Concentration, strength and dexterity can all be encouraged by constructional toys such as this wooden set made by Galt Toys.
Above: This sturdy wooden posting box by ESA encourages both hand co-ordination and observation of colour and shape. At the same time, children have the fun of discovering the posted shapes in the drawer below.
Right: The ESA Variplay Triangle set is an excellent item of indoor/outdoor equipment. It offers great opportunity for group play in a variety of balancing, riding and climbing activities and costs considerably less than a conventional wooden climbing frame.

two to three year old into a house, castle, fort or space ship. This is also the age of hectic **bathtime play** and here almost anything will do: plastics cups, a watering can and plenty of floating toys will certainly extend the daily bath time routine, but it is important to encourage confidence in the water and it is a good way of coping with excess energy before bed time. Finally, although most play activities at this time are staged on the floor, the two-and-a-half to three year old is beginning to enjoy sitting at a table and concentrating, for a short time, on drawing, painting or modelling. He will find thick **wax crayons,** stubby **brushes** and short **felt markers** much easier to cope with than conventional artists' materials and will also need a plentiful supply of paper. I have found sheets of newspaper perfectly adequate for voracious scribblers and considerably cheaper than special paper.

Three to five years

Play time activity is now a shared pursuit—one in which the adult world is imitated with increasing absorption and accuracy. Conflicts, adjustments, difficulties and emotional problems can also be acted out in many disguises through dressing up, climbing, drawing and painting. In a play house, hospital, shop or theatre a child can express his anxieties and voice them in a way that he could never do in real life. Equipment for such play must, therefore, relate to real-life situations and experiences. A basket of dressing up clothes, a set of workman-like tools, transport toys of all kinds, model farms, a doll's house or

Left: Storyboard—a three-dimensional teaching aid, designed by John Ryall of the London College of Furniture in co-operation with speech therapists at the Newcomen Centre, Guy's Hospital, London.

play-shop, painting materials and drawing equipment—these should be the contents of the three-to-five year old's toy cupboard. At the same time, confidence in movement and balance leads to active as well as imaginative play on climbing equipment—'Look how high I am' is teamed with 'this is my castle/mountain/tree house'. Increasing visual awareness leads to first steps in reading and an ever-increasing vocabulary is used to translate the imaginary world into lively reality. At this stage, it is dangerous to be dogmatic and specific about play equipment, since this is when individual skills and aptitudes come to the fore. Certainly, it would seem that toys can often be divided too strictly into boy and girl categories. The four year old girl may well be imitating her mother, primarily through playing with dolls whereas a four year old boy is more likely to be preoccupied with cars, trucks, tool kits and construction sets, but no rules apply here.

The important thing to remember is that toys must be *durable.* A broken truck wheel or limbless doll do not merely mean money lost on repairs or replacement. To a child they symbolise frustration and disappointment, as well as a loss of confidence in the intrinsic value of his possessions. You should also remember that the younger the child, the larger the toy. Young children can cope with, and are impressed by, large scale toys, whereas later on they will enjoy handling and playing with small things. Equally, if a toy is designed to move, then they like to be its driving force themselves and are quickly bored by watching mechanical toys, however colourful and noisy. Finally, do not attempt to steer or direct a child who is absorbed in a play activity. Let him make his own decisions and discoveries and only help when asked. Your reward will be a personal, imaginative interpretation of a game.

Parties

In my experience, the success of any children's party largely depends on the amount of work you put into it beforehand. Guest and shopping lists must be drawn up; food must be bought and prepared in advance in order to leave you free on the day to clear the room, blow up the balloons, plan the entertainment, wrap up presents and generally prepare yourself for what will certainly be a hectic afternoon.

Under threes

Although children aged less than three may not mix or play together very much, most young children like dressing up and a party atmosphere is enjoyed at any age. Move the furniture against the wall, bring out the largest toys you have and, if possible, arrange to borrow a rocking horse, indoor swing or slide—then let the children play on their own. Tea time poses more problems. Ideally, you need one high-chair per child to avoid inevitable spills and indignant cries of 'who's been eating *my* crisps' or 'John has taken *my* biscuit!' Still, it is unlikely that you can provide enough suitable chairs, so the best answer is to spread a large protective sheet on the floor and give each child his or her own 'basket' of food. These can be made from sheets of folded card paper with a handle looped over the top, secured at the sides with staples. In this way each child has his own picnic-style food supply and will, with luck, remain stationary until tea is over. The protective sheet is essential so that, at the end of the day, all the tea party debris can be emptied straight into the dustbin and the sheet tossed into the washing machine. If your child's birthday occurs during the summer months, an outdoor garden party will obviously save a lot of time, trouble and clearing up afterwards. One of the best parties for two year olds I have ever been to was centred on a convenient pile of earth, left by builders at work on an indoor house conversion, which occupied half a dozen small guests for the entire afternoon. You cannot rely on the British climate though, so even if the day looks promising, you should always be prepared for a hasty retreat indoors.

Three to five year olds

Children are great traditionalists and you will find that a simple formula of non-stop entertainment, a delicious tea and a take-home present cannot fail. You can expect most children from the age of three years to enjoy lively party games, such as 'Musical Bumps', Pass the Parcel' or 'Here we go round the mulberry bush' —but not for long. So be prepared for a rapid change of activities and have all the party props ready. If you have to spend ten minutes hunting for a suitable record or a packet of Smarties the day may be lost. As with adult parties, the worst moments are the first, so start with a lively game which newcomers can join in as they arrive. For example, 'Pinning the Tail on the Donkey' is an excellent ice-breaker for most age groups. A word of warning, however, on prize-winning party games in general. The young ones may not understand the concept of competitive games ending in a single reward, so you may have to console the disappointed with a rapid change to something rather less exacting, like 'Ring-a-Ring-a-Roses', or 'Oranges and Lemons.' In any case, since the majority of good party games need musical accompaniment a record player or piano is an essential item of children's party equipment, and the music should be lively, rhythmical and, above all, familiar. Popular musical games include 'Musical Bumps,' 'The Farmer's in his Den,' 'Nuts in May' and some lesser known ones which will no doubt be familiar to playgroup goers, such as 'If You are Happy and You Know it Clap your Hands . . . stamp your feet . . . nod your head' . . . and any other variations you care to name. Finally, 'Passing the Parcel' is a good pre-tea-time activity for the whole group.

Food for parties

Children are as fastidious as adults when it comes to party food. No birthday party is complete without a cake and candles and I have found that a chocolate sponge with plenty of chocolate butter icing is a perennial favourite. Other delicacies include a plentiful supply of crisps, small sausages on sticks, Marmite sandwiches and cheese straws, with chocolate biscuits or crackers, gingerbread men, jelly and icecream to finish with. The food should also look decorative and here a lot depends on table layout and accessories. Paper plates and cups are obviously a good solution to creating a colourful-looking table-setting with no risk of breakages, and you can now buy tough paper cloths with matching plates and beakers in bright primary colours and patterns. To avoid the otherwise inevitable rush and confusion over seating arrangements, label each place with the guests' initials—even three year olds can distinguish their initial letters— and you can then call the children individually into tea by announcing 'Whose name begins with A? E?' . . . and so on.

Conclusion

However well you plan your parties in advance, you are almost certainly going to be faced at the end of the day with a confusion of squashed jellies, discarded wrapping papers and a band of over-excited children.

Similarly, the advice in this book cannot possibly hope to prevent much of the noise and intermittent chaos that goes with living with young children. But everyday tasks can be made easier by planning ahead and organising your space with care *before* your first child arrives and by buying only essential equipment that will function efficiently and last for a long time.

This is advice that will always be useful and is not limited to planning your home to cope with young children. When you finally send your five year olds off to school you will need to reorganise your home to cope with their changing needs. As they grow older, for example, the playroom nursery will need to provide for quieter activities such as reading and homework, as well as for indoor hobbies and lively entertaining sessions with friends.

Later still, you may even consider extending your house to provide them with the further independence of a self-contained flat or bedsitter. Whatever your budget or capabilities, the principles of planning and design in this book should help you to adapt your home to to meet these changing needs and demands.

Acknowledgements

Photographs

Page 7
La Maison de Marie Claire
Photography Marcel Duffas
Supplied by Camera Press, London

Page 8
Supplied by The Royal Society
for the Prevention of Accidents

Page 18
Photography Photos Godeaut
Supplied by Sungravure Syndication

Page 25
Left and top right
Photography David Cripps
Room painted by Martin Sharp

Bottom right
Photography Spike Powell
Supplied by the Elizabeth Whiting
Picture Agency

Page 27
Left
Photography Rob Matheson

Right
Photography Tim Street-Porter
Supplied by the Elizabeth Whiting
Picture Agency

Page 32
Photography Graham Henderson
Supplied by the Elizabeth Whiting
Picture Agency

Page 39
Bottom row
Photography Jane Bown
Originally for The Observer
Colour Magazine

Page 40
Supplied by The Pre-School
Playgroups Association

Page 64
Photography Colin Curwood

Photographs also supplied by the
following manufacturers
ESA Creative Learning Limited
Galt Toys
Kiddicraft
Mothercare
Placemakers USA

Index